NIGERIA'S DOOM

The Curse of Political

Patronage How Nigeria's

Elites Sustain Corruption and

Inequality

Copyright Page:

Copyright © [2024] by [MIRIAM OKOROIWU]

All rights reserved. No part of this publication may be reproduced, distributed, or transmitted in any form or by any means, including photocopying, recording, or other electronic or mechanical methods, without the prior written permission of the publisher, except in the case of brief quotations embodied in critical reviews and certain other noncommercial uses permitted by copyright law.

- Introduction: 4
- CHTAPTER ONE 6
  - *Corruption Chronicles: Unraveling Nigeria's Downfall* 6
- CHAPTER TWO 9
  - *Failed Promises: The Story of Nigeria's Broken Governance* 9
- CHAPTER THREE 12
  - *Resource Curse: Oil, Wealth, and Nigeria's Tragic Fate* 12
- CHAPTER FOUR 15
  - *Ethnic Divide: Exploring Nigeria's Fragmented Society* 15
- CHAPTER FIVE 18
  - *Boko Haram: Terror and Tragedy in Nigeria* 18
- CHAPTER SIX 21
  - *Environmental Crisis: Degradation and Disaster in Nigeria* 21
- CHAPTER SEVEN 24
  - *Youth Unemployment: The Looming Crisis in Nigeria* 24
- CHAPTER EIGHT 27
  - *Infrastructure Decay: The Crumbling Foundations of Nigeria's Future* 27
- CHAPTER NINE 30
  - *Healthcare Emergency: Challenges and Failures in Nigeria* 30
- CHAPTER TEN 33
  - *Education in Peril: The Struggle for Quality Learning in Nigeria* 33
- CHAPTER ELEVEN 37
  - *Nigeria's Diaspora: Migration, Brain Drain, and Lost Potential* 37

Introduction:

In the tumultuous landscape of Nigeria's socio-political arena, a pervasive shadow looms large, casting a pall over the hopes and aspirations of its people. This shadow, known as the curse of political patronage, has entrenched itself deeply within the fabric of the nation, perpetuating a cycle of corruption, inequality, and despair. Nigeria, blessed with abundant natural resources and a vibrant populace, finds itself ensnared in a web of systemic dysfunction, wherein the interests of the few outweigh the needs of the many.

At the heart of Nigeria's woes lies the intricate network of political patronage, a system wherein powerful elites wield their influence and resources to maintain control over the levers of power. This system, built upon a foundation of nepotism and cronyism, serves as a barrier to progress, stifling economic growth, eroding public trust, and widening the gap between the ruling class and the marginalized masses.

In this exploration of Nigeria's doom, we delve into the labyrinthine corridors of power, tracing the origins of political patronage and examining its corrosive effects on the nation's institutions, economy, and social cohesion. From the embezzlement of public funds to the manipulation of electoral processes, we confront the stark realities of a nation held captive by its own elites.

Furthermore, we unravel the symbiotic relationship between political patronage and corruption, wherein the pursuit of personal gain takes precedence over the collective welfare of the Nigerian people. As resources are siphoned off into the coffers of the privileged few, essential services languish in neglect, leaving communities mired in poverty, disease, and despair.

Yet amid-st the gloom, glimmers of hope emerge, as grassroots movements and civil society organizations rally against the tide of corruption and impunity. Through their tireless efforts, they seek to dismantle the entrenched structures of patronage, reclaiming the promise of a brighter future for all Nigerians.

In the pages that follow, we embark on a journey of discovery and revelation, shining a light on the darkest corners of Nigeria's political landscape. As we confront the curse of political patronage head-on, we bear witness to the resilience of a nation determined to break free from the shackles of its own making.

CHTAPTER ONE

Corruption Chronicles: Unraveling Nigeria's Downfall

In the global arena, Nigeria is often recognized for its vast resources, vibrant culture, and resilient population. Yet, beneath the surface lies a deep-seated issue that has plagued the nation for decades: corruption. Like a corrosive force eating away at the foundations of society, corruption has been a significant contributor to Nigeria's downward spiral, hindering development, eroding trust in institutions, and perpetuating inequality. In this article, we embark on a journey to unravel the corruption chronicles that have played a pivotal role in Nigeria's downfall.

The Anatomy of Corruption

Corruption in Nigeria manifests itself in various forms, ranging from petty bribery to grand-scale embezzlement.

At its core lies the abuse of power for personal gain, with government officials, business leaders, and individuals alike engaging in practices that undermine the public good. The misappropriation of public funds, bribery to secure contracts, and favoritism in appointments are just a few examples of how corruption permeates every level of society.

The Impact on Development

The consequences of corruption are far-reaching and profound, stifling economic growth, exacerbating poverty, and undermining efforts to improve living standards. Despite being one of the wealthiest nations in Africa in terms of natural resources, Nigeria continues to grapple with widespread poverty and inadequate infrastructure. The diversion of funds meant for essential services like healthcare, education, and infrastructure into the pockets of corrupt officials has deprived millions of Nigerians of the basic necessities of life.

Erosion of Trust and Confidence

Corruption also erodes trust in government institutions and undermines the rule of law, creating a climate of impunity where the powerful act with impunity while the vulnerable suffer the consequences. Citizens lose faith in the ability of the government to serve their interests, leading to disenchantment, apathy, and in some cases, civil unrest. The perception of corruption as a pervasive and insurmountable problem further undermines efforts to foster transparency, accountability, and good governance.

The Road to Redemption

Addressing corruption in Nigeria requires a multifaceted approach that targets both the supply and demand sides of corruption. Strengthening anti-corruption laws and institutions, promoting transparency and accountability, and fostering a culture of integrity are essential steps in the fight against corruption. Equally important is the need to address the underlying socioeconomic factors that fuel corruption, such as poverty, inequality, and lack of access to education and opportunities.

Nigeria stands at a crossroads, grappling with the profound consequences of decades of corruption. However, amid-st the challenges lies the opportunity for renewal and redemption. By confronting corruption head-on, Nigeria can unlock its full potential, harnessing its abundant resources and talent to build a more prosperous and equitable society. It is only through collective action, political will, and unwavering commitment that Nigeria can overcome the corruption chronicles that have contributed to its downfall and chart a course towards a brighter future.

CHAPTER TWO

Failed Promises: The Story of Nigeria's Broken Governance

In the tapestry of Nigeria's history, there are threads woven with the promises of progress, prosperity, and equitable governance. Yet, as time unfurls, it becomes painfully evident that many of these promises remain unfulfilled, leaving behind a trail of disappointment, disillusionment, and despair. This article delves into the narrative of Nigeria's broken governance, examining the factors that have contributed to its failure and the implications for the nation's present and future.

A Legacy of Unmet Expectations

Since gaining independence from colonial rule in 1960, Nigeria has witnessed a succession of leaders who have pledged to usher in an era of development, democracy, and social justice. However, for many Nigerians, these promises have remained elusive, overshadowed by pervasive corruption, political instability, and economic mismanagement. Despite being blessed with abundant natural resources and a talented workforce, Nigeria continues to lag behind its peers in key indicators of human development, with millions living in poverty and struggling to access basic services.

Corruption: The Cancer of Governance

At the heart of Nigeria's governance woes lies the scourge of corruption, which has permeated every level of society, from the corridors of power to the grassroots. The diversion of public funds meant for development projects into private pockets, nepotism in appointments, and the subversion of the rule of law have all contributed to the erosion of trust in government institutions and the perpetuation of inequality. Despite efforts to combat corruption, including the establishment of anti-corruption agencies and the passage of anti-corruption laws, progress has been slow, and impunity remains rampant.

Political Instability and Ethnic Divisions

Nigeria's governance challenges are further compounded by political instability and deep-seated ethnic divisions, which have fueled tensions and hindered efforts to foster national unity. The country's federal structure, comprising a diverse array of ethnic groups and regions, has often been a source of contention, with competing interests vying for power and resources. The prevalence of identity politics, coupled with a winner-takes-all mentality, has stymied efforts to build consensus and promote inclusive governance, exacerbating social divisions and hindering progress.

The Way Forward: A Call for Reform

Despite the myriad challenges facing Nigeria's governance system, there remains hope for reform and renewal. Key to this is a commitment to transparency, accountability, and the rule of law, which are essential pillars of effective governance. Strengthening democratic institutions, empowering civil society, and promoting civic engagement are also critical steps in fostering a culture of participatory governance and holding leaders accountable to the people they serve. Moreover, addressing the root causes of corruption, including poverty, inequality, and lack of access to education and opportunities, is essential to building a more just and equitable society.

As Nigeria grapples with the legacy of failed promises and broken governance, the need for reform has never been more urgent. By confronting the challenges head-on, fostering dialogue and cooperation, and embracing the principles of transparency, accountability, and inclusivity, Nigeria can begin to chart a new course towards a brighter future. It is only through collective action, political will, and a steadfast commitment to the common good that Nigeria can fulfill the promises of its independence and realize its full potential as a prosperous and thriving nation.

CHAPTER THREE

Resource Curse: Oil, Wealth, and Nigeria's Tragic Fate

Nigeria, often hailed as the "Giant of Africa," possesses abundant natural resources, with oil being the crown jewel of its economic landscape. However, beneath the veneer of wealth lies a sobering reality: the resource curse. This article delves into the intricate dynamics of Nigeria's oil-dependent economy, exploring how the nation's vast oil wealth has paradoxically become a source of tragedy rather than triumph.

The Promise of Oil Wealth

When oil was discovered in commercial quantities in Nigeria in the 1950s, it was hailed as a harbinger of prosperity and development. The newfound wealth promised to fuel economic growth, create jobs, and lift millions out of poverty. However, as history has shown, the reality has been far more complex, with Nigeria's oil wealth often serving as a double-edged sword.

The Curse Unveiled

The resource curse refers to the paradoxical phenomenon whereby countries rich in natural resources, particularly oil and minerals, often experience slower economic growth, increased poverty, and heightened levels of corruption and conflict. Nigeria exemplifies this curse in many ways. Despite being one of the largest oil producers in Africa and the world, the majority of its population continues to live in poverty, with basic infrastructure and social services sorely lacking.

Corruption and Mismanagement

At the heart of Nigeria's resource curse lies the toxic combination of corruption and mismanagement. The opaque nature of the oil industry, coupled with weak governance structures and institutional deficiencies, has created fertile ground for corruption to flourish. Billions of dollars in oil revenue have been squandered through embezzlement, kickbacks, and fraudulent contracts, depriving the country of much-needed resources for development.

Environmental Degradation and Social Displacement

The extraction and production of oil in Nigeria have also taken a heavy toll on the environment and local communities. Oil spills, gas flaring, and pollution have led to widespread environmental degradation, contaminating water sources, destroying ecosystems, and jeopardizing public health. Moreover, the displacement of indigenous communities to make way for oil exploration and infrastructure projects has fueled social unrest and conflict, exacerbating the already precarious socioeconomic situation.

Breaking the Curse: A Path Forward

Breaking free from the resource curse requires bold and comprehensive reforms that address the root causes of Nigeria's woes. This includes strengthening governance and accountability mechanisms, promoting transparency in the oil sector, and diversifying the economy away from over-reliance on oil. Furthermore, prioritizing investments in human capital development, infrastructure, and sustainable development initiatives can help ensure that the benefits of Nigeria's natural resources are shared equitably among its citizens.

As Nigeria grapples with the tragic consequences of the resource curse, the need for reform has never been more pressing. By learning from past mistakes, fostering inclusive and sustainable development, and embracing good governance principles, Nigeria can begin to break free from the shackles of its oil-dependent economy. It is only through concerted efforts and a steadfast commitment to the common good that Nigeria can rewrite its destiny and realize its full potential as a prosperous and thriving nation.

CHAPTER FOUR

Ethnic Divide: Exploring Nigeria's Fragmented Society

Nigeria, with its diverse cultural tapestry and multitude of ethnic groups, stands as a microcosm of Africa's rich and complex heritage. However, beneath the surface of this diversity lies a fault line that has long threatened the nation's stability and unity: the ethnic divide. In this article, we delve into the nuances of Nigeria's fragmented society, examining the historical, social, and political factors that have contributed to ethnic tensions and divisions.

A Tapestry of Diversity

Nigeria is home to over 250 ethnic groups, each with its own language, culture, and traditions. From the Hausa-Fulani in the north to the Yoruba in the southwest and the Igbo in the southeast, Nigeria's ethnic landscape is as varied as it is vibrant. This diversity has long been celebrated as a source of strength, but it has also been a source of tension and conflict, particularly when ethnic identities are politicized and exploited for personal gain.

Historical Roots of Division

The seeds of Nigeria's ethnic divide were sown during the colonial era, when British colonialists imposed arbitrary borders and administrative structures that often ignored ethnic and cultural boundaries. This legacy of colonialism laid the groundwork for ethnic tensions, as different groups vied for power, resources, and recognition within the newly formed nation-state. Furthermore, the legacy of colonialism also fostered a sense of distrust and resentment between ethnic groups, which persists to this day.

Political Exploitation and Identity Politics

In the post-independence era, Nigeria's ethnic diversity became a potent tool for political manipulation, as politicians sought to mobilize support along ethnic lines to consolidate power. The politics of ethnicity, characterized by patronage, nepotism, and favoritism towards one's ethnic group, have contributed to a sense of marginalization and exclusion among minority groups. Moreover, the winner-takes-all mentality that pervades Nigerian politics has further exacerbated ethnic tensions, as groups vie for control of scarce resources and political power.

Socioeconomic Disparities

Ethnic divisions in Nigeria are often intertwined with socioeconomic disparities, with certain ethnic groups enjoying greater access to education, employment, and economic opportunities than others. This has led to feelings of resentment and alienation among marginalized communities, who perceive themselves as being left behind in the race for development and prosperity. Moreover, economic inequalities along ethnic lines have fueled perceptions of injustice and discrimination, further deepening the divide.

Toward Unity and Understanding

Addressing Nigeria's ethnic divide requires a concerted effort to foster unity, understanding, and inclusivity among all ethnic groups. This includes promoting dialogue and reconciliation, celebrating Nigeria's diversity as a source of strength rather than division, and addressing the root causes of ethnic tensions, such as socioeconomic disparities and political marginalization. Furthermore, building strong institutions that promote transparency, accountability, and good governance can help mitigate the politicization of ethnicity and create a more inclusive society for all Nigerians.

As Nigeria navigates the complexities of its fragmented society, the path to unity and reconciliation may be long and arduous, but it is not insurmountable. By confronting the legacy of colonialism, addressing socioeconomic disparities, and fostering inclusive governance, Nigeria can begin to bridge the ethnic divide and forge a common identity based on shared values and aspirations. It is only through collective effort and a commitment to national unity that Nigeria can realize its full potential as a prosperous, peaceful, and united nation.

CHAPTER FIVE

Boko Haram: Terror and Tragedy in Nigeria

In the labyrinth of Nigeria's socio-political landscape, one name echoes with chilling resonance: Boko Haram. This extremist group has inflicted untold suffering upon the Nigerian people, leaving a trail of terror and tragedy in its wake. From bombings and massacres to kidnappings and forced displacements, Boko Haram's reign of violence has plunged Nigeria into a state of perpetual fear and uncertainty.

Origins and Ideology

Boko Haram, which translates roughly to "Western education is forbidden," was founded in the early 2000s by Mohammed Yusuf, a radical cleric who espoused a virulent anti-Western and anti-government ideology. The group's initial grievances centered on perceived injustices against Muslims in northern Nigeria, including poverty, corruption, and marginalization.

However, over time, Boko Haram's ideology morphed into a violent jihadist agenda, seeking to impose its radical interpretation of Islam through terror and bloodshed.

Tactics of Terror

Boko Haram's tactics are as ruthless as they are indiscriminate. Suicide bombings, ambushes, and massacres have become chillingly routine, targeting not only government institutions and security forces but also civilian populations, including schools, markets, and places of worship. The group's infamous abduction of over 200 schoolgirls from Chibok in 2014 captured the world's attention, highlighting the depths of depravity to which Boko Haram is willing to sink in its pursuit of power and control.

Humanitarian Crisis

The impact of Boko Haram's reign of terror extends far beyond the physical casualties of its attacks. The group's campaign of violence has triggered a humanitarian crisis of epic proportions, with millions of Nigerians displaced from their homes and communities torn apart by fear and suspicion. Human rights abuses, including forced conscription, sexual violence, and the use of child soldiers, have further compounded the suffering of those caught in the crossfire.

Government Response and Regional Cooperation

Nigeria's government has struggled to contain the Boko Haram insurgency, facing criticism for its perceived inability to protect its citizens and root out the group's leadership. Military offensives and counterinsurgency operations have met with limited success, while efforts to address the underlying grievances driving recruitment to Boko Haram have been slow to materialize. However, regional cooperation, particularly with neighboring countries like Chad, Niger, and Cameroon, has shown promise in disrupting Boko Haram's operations and curtailing its ability to launch cross-border attacks.

The Road Ahead

As Nigeria grapples with the ongoing threat posed by Boko Haram, the road ahead remains fraught with challenges and uncertainties. Addressing the root causes of extremism, including poverty, corruption, and marginalization, is essential to preventing the emergence of new generations of militants. Moreover, investing in education, job creation, and community resilience can help inoculate vulnerable populations against the lure of violent extremism. Ultimately, defeating Boko Haram will require not only military action but also a comprehensive strategy that addresses the socioeconomic, political, and ideological dimensions of the conflict.

Boko Haram's reign of terror has left an indelible mark on Nigeria, inflicting untold suffering upon its people and plunging the nation into a state of crisis. However, amid-st the tragedy and despair, there remains hope for a brighter future. By confronting the root causes of extremism, fostering regional cooperation, and investing in community resilience, Nigeria can begin to heal the wounds inflicted by Boko Haram and build a more peaceful and prosperous society for all its citizens.

CHAPTER SIX

Environmental Crisis: Degradation and Disaster in Nigeria

Nigeria, with its diverse ecosystems and rich natural resources, is facing an environmental crisis of alarming proportions. From deforestation and pollution to climate change and oil spills, the degradation of Nigeria's environment poses a grave threat to the health, livelihoods, and future of its people. In this article, we explore the multifaceted dimensions of the environmental crisis gripping Nigeria and the urgent need for action to mitigate its devastating impact.

Oil Pollution: A Toxic Legacy

The discovery of oil in Nigeria was heralded as a boon for the nation's economy, promising wealth and prosperity for its people. However, the extraction and production of oil have come at a steep cost to the environment and public health. Decades of oil spills, leaks, and gas flaring have contaminated water sources, destroyed ecosystems, and devastated communities in Nigeria's oil-producing regions, particularly in the Niger Delta. Despite efforts to hold oil companies accountable for environmental damage, impunity remains widespread, leaving affected communities to bear the brunt of the toxic legacy of Nigeria's oil industry.

Deforestation and Desertification

Nigeria's forests, once teeming with biodiversity, are rapidly disappearing due to deforestation and unsustainable land use practices. Logging, agricultural expansion, and urbanization have all contributed to the loss of forest cover, exacerbating soil erosion, loss of habitat, and biodiversity decline. In addition, the encroachment of the Sahara Desert in Nigeria's northern regions is exacerbating desertification, threatening agricultural productivity and exacerbating food insecurity in already vulnerable communities.

Pollution and Public Health

The degradation of Nigeria's environment has serious implications for public health, with pollution from industrial activities, waste disposal, and vehicular emissions contributing to respiratory illnesses, waterborne diseases, and other health problems. Poor sanitation infrastructure and inadequate access to clean water exacerbate the health risks faced by millions of Nigerians, particularly in urban slums and informal settlements where environmental pollution is most acute.

Climate Change: A Gathering Storm

The impacts of climate change, including rising temperatures, erratic rainfall patterns, and extreme weather events, are further compounding Nigeria's environmental woes. Flooding, droughts, and heatwaves are becoming more frequent and severe, leading to crop failures, displacement, and loss of livelihoods for millions of Nigerians. Moreover, Nigeria's vulnerability to climate change is exacerbated by its limited capacity to adapt and mitigate the effects of global warming, highlighting the urgent need for investment in climate-resilient infrastructure and sustainable development initiatives.

Toward Sustainable Solutions

Addressing Nigeria's environmental crisis requires a multifaceted approach that addresses the root causes of degradation while promoting sustainable development and resilience. This includes strengthening environmental regulations and enforcement mechanisms, investing in renewable energy and clean technologies, and promoting sustainable land management and conservation practices. Moreover, fostering public awareness and community engagement is essential to mobilizing collective action and building a culture of environmental stewardship among Nigerians.

Nigeria stands at a critical juncture in its environmental journey, grappling with the consequences of decades of unsustainable development and neglect. However, amidst the challenges lie opportunities for transformation and renewal. By prioritizing environmental protection, promoting sustainable development, and embracing climate resilience, Nigeria can chart a course towards a more prosperous, equitable, and sustainable future for all its citizens. It is only through collective action, political will, and a steadfast commitment to the preservation of

Nigeria's natural heritage that the environmental crisis facing the nation can be addressed and overcome.

CHAPTER SEVEN

Youth Unemployment: The Looming Crisis in Nigeria

In Nigeria, a demographic bulge is poised to either propel the nation into a future of boundless opportunity or plunge it into the depths of despair. At the heart of this dichotomy lies the issue of youth unemployment, a ticking time bomb that threatens to unravel the social fabric and undermine the prospects of a generation brimming with potential. In this article, we delve into the complexities of youth unemployment in Nigeria, exploring its root causes, far-reaching consequences, and the urgent need for action to avert a looming crisis.

The Youth Bulge: A Double-Edged Sword

Nigeria boasts one of the largest youth populations in the world, with young people under the age of 35 accounting for over 60% of the total population. On one hand, this demographic dividend holds the promise of a dynamic and vibrant workforce capable of driving economic growth, innovation, and social progress. However, on the other hand, the failure to harness the potential of Nigeria's youth risks squandering this demographic dividend and perpetuating a cycle of poverty, inequality, and social unrest.

Root Causes of Youth Unemployment

The factors contributing to youth unemployment in Nigeria are manifold and interconnected. Structural issues such as inadequate education and skills training, limited access to finance and credit, and a lack of job opportunities in key sectors of the economy exacerbate the problem. Moreover, systemic challenges including corruption, inefficiency, and poor governance further hinder efforts to address youth unemployment and create an enabling environment for economic growth and job creation.

Consequences of Youth Unemployment

The consequences of youth unemployment extend far beyond the individual level, impacting families, communities, and the nation as a whole. Economic stagnation, social unrest, and political instability are among the potential outcomes of a large and disillusioned youth population deprived of opportunities for meaningful employment and social mobility. Moreover, the specter of youth unemployment threatens to undermine Nigeria's efforts to achieve sustainable development and realize its full potential as a prosperous and inclusive society.

The Way Forward: A Call to Action

Addressing youth unemployment in Nigeria requires a comprehensive and coordinated response that addresses the root causes of the problem while fostering an environment conducive to job creation and economic growth. Investing in education and skills development, promoting entrepreneurship and innovation, and supporting small and medium-sized enterprises (SMEs) are essential steps in empowering young people to unlock their full potential and contribute to the nation's development. Moreover, tackling corruption, improving governance, and fostering transparency and accountability are critical for creating a level playing field and restoring trust in public institutions.

As Nigeria grapples with the looming crisis of youth unemployment, the need for action has never been more urgent. By harnessing the energy, creativity, and talents of its young people, Nigeria can unlock a future of prosperity, stability, and inclusive growth. However, achieving this vision requires bold and decisive leadership, sustained investment in youth development, and a commitment to addressing the root causes of unemployment and inequality. It is only through collective effort and shared responsibility that Nigeria can realize its aspirations and build a better future for generations to come.

CHAPTER EIGHT

Infrastructure Decay: The Crumbling Foundations of Nigeria's Future

In the tapestry of Nigeria's development journey, the state of its infrastructure stands as a poignant reflection of its progress and challenges. Yet, beneath the gleaming skyscrapers of its urban centers and the bustling highways of its major cities lies a stark reality: the decay of infrastructure. In this article, we delve into the depths of Nigeria's infrastructure crisis, exploring its root causes, far-reaching consequences, and the imperative need for action to avert a looming catastrophe.

A Legacy of Neglect

Decades of under-investment, mismanagement, and neglect have taken a heavy toll on Nigeria's infrastructure, with roads, bridges, power plants, and water supply systems crumbling under the weight of decay and disrepair. The failure to maintain and upgrade infrastructure assets has not only hindered economic growth and productivity but has also endangered the safety and well-being of millions of Nigerians who rely on these essential services for their daily lives.

Transportation Gridlock

The state of Nigeria's transportation infrastructure is emblematic of the broader crisis facing the nation. Congested roads, potholed highways, and dilapidated bridges make travel a perilous and time-consuming endeavor, stifling economic activity and hampering mobility. In urban centers like Lagos, gridlock is a daily ordeal, with commuters spending hours stuck in traffic jams that choke the life out of the city and sap its vitality.

Power Outages and Energy Shortages

Nigeria's energy infrastructure is similarly plagued by chronic deficiencies and inefficiencies. Frequent power outages, voltage fluctuations, and energy shortages are a grim reality for many Nigerians, stifling economic growth, undermining productivity, and hindering the delivery of essential services. Despite abundant natural resources, including oil and gas, Nigeria's energy sector remains hamstrung by outdated infrastructure, inadequate investment, and institutional bottlenecks.

Water and Sanitation Crisis

Access to clean water and sanitation facilities is another pressing challenge facing Nigeria's infrastructure sector. Millions of Nigerians lack access to safe drinking water and proper sanitation, leading to widespread health problems, including waterborne diseases and malnutrition. The decay of water supply systems, coupled with poor waste management practices, exacerbates environmental pollution and public health risks, posing a formidable barrier to Nigeria's development aspirations.

The Urgent Need for Action

Addressing Nigeria's infrastructure decay requires a concerted and sustained effort to invest in maintenance, rehabilitation, and modernization initiatives. Prioritizing infrastructure development, improving project planning and execution, and enhancing regulatory frameworks are essential steps in revitalizing Nigeria's infrastructure sector and laying the foundations for sustainable growth and development. Moreover, fostering public-private partnerships, attracting foreign investment, and leveraging innovative financing mechanisms can help bridge the infrastructure gap and unlock new opportunities for economic prosperity and social progress.

As Nigeria confronts the monumental challenge of infrastructure decay, the stakes could not be higher. The future of the nation hinges on its ability to build and maintain the infrastructure needed to support a growing population, drive economic growth, and enhance the quality of life for all Nigerians. By prioritizing infrastructure investment, fostering innovation, and strengthening governance and accountability, Nigeria can overcome the obstacles standing in its path and build a brighter future for generations to come. It is only through collective action, bold leadership, and unwavering commitment that Nigeria can realize its potential and thrive in the 21st century.

CHAPTER NINE

Healthcare Emergency: Challenges and Failures in Nigeria

In the complex tapestry of Nigeria's development landscape, the state of its healthcare system stands as a stark reflection of both progress and persistent challenges. Despite notable achievements in certain areas, Nigeria continues to grapple with a healthcare emergency characterized by a myriad of obstacles, shortcomings, and failures. In this article, we explore the multifaceted dimensions of Nigeria's healthcare crisis, examining its root causes, far-reaching consequences, and the imperative need for trans-formative action.

A System in Crisis

Nigeria's healthcare system is besieged by a host of structural deficiencies, institutional weaknesses, and resource constraints that undermine its ability to meet the needs of its population. Inadequate funding, a shortage of trained healthcare professionals, and a lack of essential medical equipment and supplies are just a few of the challenges facing Nigeria's healthcare infrastructure. Moreover, disparities in access to healthcare between urban and rural areas, as well as between different socioeconomic groups, exacerbate inequalities and exacerbate the burden of disease for the most vulnerable segments of the population.

The Burden of Disease

Nigeria's healthcare crisis is compounded by the burden of communicable and non-communicable diseases that afflict millions of Nigerians and strain the capacity of the healthcare system. Infectious diseases such as malaria, tuberculosis, and HIV/AIDS continue to exact a heavy toll on the population, particularly in rural areas where access to healthcare is limited. At the same time, the prevalence of non-communicable diseases such as diabetes, hypertension, and cancer is on the rise, further stretching the resources and capabilities of Nigeria's healthcare infrastructure.

Maternal and Child Health

Maternal and child health is another area of concern in Nigeria, with high rates of maternal and infant mortality that far exceed global averages. Limited access to prenatal care, skilled birth attendants, and emergency obstetric services contribute to preventable deaths among mothers and children, perpetuating a cycle of inter-generational poverty and poor health outcomes. Moreover, cultural and socioeconomic factors often impede efforts to improve maternal and child health, including early marriage, gender discrimination, and lack of education.

The Role of Governance and Leadership

The challenges facing Nigeria's healthcare system are not insurmountable, but they require bold leadership, effective governance, and sustained investment to address. Strengthening health systems, expanding access to essential services, and improving the quality of care are essential steps in building a more resilient and responsive healthcare system that can meet the needs of all Nigerians. Moreover, addressing the root causes of poor health, including poverty, inequality, and lack of education, is critical for achieving sustainable progress and improving health outcomes for the entire population.

Nigeria's healthcare emergency demands urgent attention and concerted action from government leaders, policymakers, healthcare professionals, and civil society stakeholders alike. By prioritizing healthcare investment, strengthening health systems, and addressing the root causes of poor health, Nigeria can begin to build a more inclusive, equitable, and resilient healthcare system that delivers better health outcomes for all Nigerians. It is only through collective effort, political will, and a commitment to health as a fundamental human right that Nigeria can overcome the challenges facing its healthcare sector and pave the way for a healthier, more prosperous future.

CHAPTER TEN

Education in Peril: The Struggle for Quality Learning in Nigeria

Education has long been hailed as the cornerstone of development, empowering individuals, transforming societies, and driving economic progress. However, in Nigeria, the promise of quality education remains elusive for millions of children and youth who are trapped in a system plagued by myriad challenges, deficiencies, and failures. In this article, we explore the precarious state of education in Nigeria, examining the root causes of its perilous condition, the far-reaching consequences for the nation's future, and the urgent need for reform to ensure access to quality learning for all.

The Promise of Education

Education is often viewed as the great equalizer, offering a pathway to opportunity and empowerment for individuals regardless of their background or circumstances. In Nigeria, however, access to quality education remains a distant dream for many, particularly those living in marginalized and under-served communities. Despite significant progress in increasing enrollment rates in recent years, the quality of education in Nigeria continues to lag behind international standards, with high dropout rates, low literacy levels, and poor learning outcomes plaguing the system.

Systemic Challenges

The challenges facing Nigeria's education system are multifaceted and deeply entrenched, rooted in decades of under-investment, mismanagement, and neglect. Inadequate funding, a shortage of qualified teachers, overcrowded classrooms, and a lack of basic infrastructure are just a few of the obstacles hindering the delivery of quality education to Nigerian children. Moreover, disparities in access to education between urban and rural areas, as well as between different socioeconomic groups, exacerbate inequalities and perpetuate a cycle of poverty and underachievement.

Curriculum Relevance and Quality

Another critical issue facing Nigeria's education system is the relevance and quality of the curriculum. Outdated textbooks, rote memorization, and a lack of practical skills training contribute to a disconnect between what students learn in school and the skills they need to succeed in the 21st-century economy. Moreover, the emphasis on high-stakes examinations and standardized testing places undue pressure on students and teachers alike, stifling creativity, critical thinking, and innovation in the classroom.

The Impact of COVID-19

The COVID-19 pandemic has further exacerbated the challenges facing Nigeria's education system, disrupting learning for millions of students and exacerbating existing inequalities. School closures, inadequate access to remote learning technologies, and disruptions to the academic calendar have widened the gap between privileged and disadvantaged students, threatening to undo decades of progress in expanding access to education. Moreover, the socioeconomic fallout of the pandemic has pushed many families deeper into poverty, making it even more difficult for children to return to school once restrictions are lifted.

The Way Forward

Addressing the crisis in Nigeria's education system requires a comprehensive and multi-dimensional approach that addresses the root causes of its deficiencies while fostering a culture of innovation, excellence, and inclusivity. This includes increasing investment in education, recruiting and training qualified teachers, improving the quality and relevance of the curriculum, and leveraging technology to enhance teaching and learning outcomes. Moreover, addressing socioeconomic barriers to education, such as poverty, gender discrimination, and lack of infrastructure, is essential for ensuring that all Nigerian children have access to quality learning opportunities.

Education is the key to unlocking Nigeria's full potential and building a brighter future for generations to come. However, achieving this vision requires bold leadership, political will, and a commitment to trans-formative change. By prioritizing education investment, strengthening governance and accountability, and fostering partnerships between government, civil society, and the private sector, Nigeria can overcome the challenges facing its education system and ensure that every child has the opportunity to fulfill their potential and contribute to the nation's development. It is only through collective effort and shared commitment that Nigeria can realize its aspirations for quality learning and inclusive education for all.

CHAPTER ELEVEN

Nigeria's Diaspora: Migration, Brain Drain, and Lost Potential

The story of Nigeria's diaspora is a tale of two worlds: the promise of opportunity and prosperity abroad juxtaposed with the loss of talent and potential at home. As millions of Nigerians seek better prospects abroad, the nation grapples with the consequences of brain drain and the challenges of harnessing the talents and contributions of its diaspora. In this article, we explore the complex dynamics of Nigeria's diaspora, examining the factors driving migration, the impacts of brain drain, and the potential for diaspora engagement in the nation's development journey.

The Pull of Opportunity

The decision to migrate is often driven by a quest for better opportunities, whether economic, educational, or professional. For many Nigerians, the allure of greener pastures abroad, with the promise of higher wages, better living standards, and access to quality education and healthcare, proves irresistible. Moreover, political instability, insecurity, and lack of economic opportunities at home further fuel the desire to seek a better life elsewhere, leading to significant levels of emigration from Nigeria to countries around the world.

Brain Drain and Lost Potential

While migration offers opportunities for individual advancement, it also carries a heavy cost for Nigeria, in the form of brain drain and loss of human capital. Highly skilled professionals, including doctors, engineers, scientists, and academics, are among those most likely to emigrate, leaving behind gaps in critical sectors of the economy and depriving Nigeria of the talent and expertise needed for sustainable development. Moreover, the departure of young, educated Nigerians exacerbates the challenge of youth unemployment and perpetuates a cycle of dependency on remittances rather than investment in domestic capacity-building.

The Paradox of Diaspora Engagement

Despite the challenges of brain drain, Nigeria's diaspora also represents a potential source of strength and resilience for the nation. Remittances sent by Nigerians abroad play a vital role in supporting household incomes, reducing poverty, and improving access to education and healthcare for millions of Nigerians. Moreover, diaspora communities often serve as ambassadors for Nigeria, promoting the nation's culture, values, and interests on the global stage and fostering connections and networks that can facilitate trade, investment, and collaboration.

Harnessing Diaspora Potential

Harnessing the potential of Nigeria's diaspora requires a concerted effort to engage with and leverage the talents, skills, and resources of Nigerians abroad for the benefit of the nation. This includes creating channels for diaspora investment, entrepreneurship, and innovation, as well as providing opportunities for diaspora professionals to contribute their expertise and knowledge to national development initiatives. Moreover, fostering a sense of belonging and connection among Nigerians abroad, through cultural exchange programs, networking events, and targeted outreach efforts, can help strengthen ties between the diaspora and Nigeria, facilitating collaboration and partnership in key areas of mutual interest.

Conclusion

Nigeria's diaspora is a complex and multifaceted phenomenon, characterized by both challenges and opportunities for the nation's development. While brain drain represents a significant loss of human capital and potential, diaspora engagement offers a pathway to resilience, innovation, and growth. By fostering dialogue, collaboration, and partnership between Nigeria and its diaspora, the nation can unlock new opportunities for sustainable development and build a brighter future for all Nigerians, both at home and abroad. It is only through inclusive and collaborative efforts that Nigeria can harness the full potential of its diaspora and realize its aspirations for prosperity, progress, and peace.

www.ingramcontent.com/pod-product-compliance
Lightning Source LLC
Chambersburg PA
CBHW070954220526
45471CB00007B/3022